GLASTONBURY, WELLS & THE LEVELS

A shortish guide

Paul White

Bossiney Books · Launceston

First published 2010 by Bossiney Books Ltd
Langore, Launceston, Cornwall PL15 8LD
www.bossineybooks.com

ISBN 978-1-906474-21-8

Printed in Great Britain by R Booth Ltd, Penryn, Cornwall

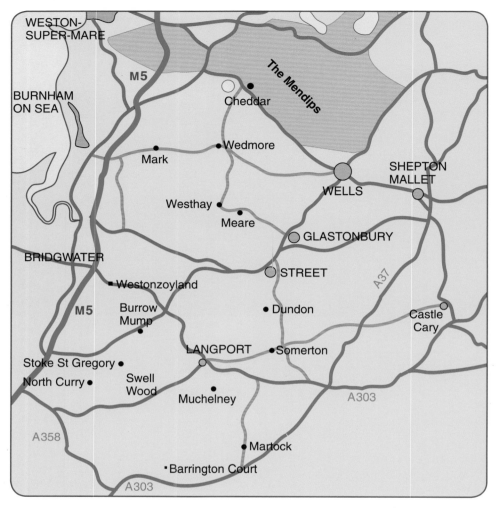

For the purpose of this book, 'the Levels' means the area bounded by the M5 to the west, by the Mendip Hills to the north and by the A37 Fosse Way and then A303 to the east and south. The coastal strip to the west of the motorway belonged historically to the Levels, but it has developed in its own way in recent times. Whilst 'the Levels' is widely accepted today as the name for the area, previous generations referred to 'the Moors'.

Acknowledgements

The map is by Nick Hawken. The cover is based on a design by Heards Design Partnership. All photographs are by the author. The author and publishers are grateful to Robert Hesketh for his additional research for this book.

How the Levels were formed

In prehistoric times, the Somerset Levels were a great fresh-water lagoon, studded with islands rising above the waters. To hunter-gatherers it was a rich environment and it was fully exploited. As early as 4000 BC, wooden trackways were being built to connect up patches of firmer ground. The famous 'Glastonbury lake villages' date from around 250 BC.

But the origin of the Levels was about 10,000 years ago, when rising sea levels at the end of the last Ice Age flooded dry land with salt water, producing a tidal swamp. A natural coastal barrier gradually developed: it took around 4000 years before fresh water predominated over salt, and reedbeds and silt gradually produced boggy wetland, some of it wooded.

The present appearance of the area is due to deliberate drainage, started by the monks of Glastonbury Abbey in the 12th century if not earlier. Within the UK this is a unique wetland landscape, though there are considerable similarities with the Cambridgeshire fens – which is probably why my wife and I feel such an affinity with it, since we lived for a number of years on the edge of the fenland.

But the Levels have largely avoided the 'agribusiness' which has impersonalised much of the fens by creating vast fields, and turned

From high points around the Levels, as here on Walton Hill, the artificial nature of the landscape can easily be seen

them into a dustbowl waiting to happen. Most of the fields in the Levels are still on a human scale; there are narrow ditches and slightly wider 'rhynes' (pronounced 'reens'), little bridges and sluices – locally called 'clyses' – and the roads are often lined by withies, alders and blackthorn hedgerows.

The reclaimed lands are, as in the fens, mostly worked from villages on the 'islands' of high ground, but these islands are both higher and more numerous than those in fenland. They contain some old houses, but fewer than you might expect. This was an area of widespread poverty. Medieval stone barns, owned by rich monasteries, may survive, but the peasants' hovels have (fortunately) been replaced.

Over the last few decades, many of the villages have acquired developments of new houses, their populations presumably now consisting mainly of commuters.

One way to envisage the shape of the Levels is to put your hands together, palms up in a begging posture, then bring your elbows together. Two cupped hollows are separated by a low ridge – the Polden Hills – and they are narrower towards the coast than inland. Your left hand is 'Sedgemoor', your right hand 'the Isle of Avalon' –

though both these names are contentious. Your right thumb represents the Mendips – but is sadly inadequate to convey the effect of what, from sea level, looks like a small mountain range.

As well as the Axe and the Parrett, the River Brue has an outlet to the sea, and they all have tributaries, most notably the Tone and the Cary. But over the last eight centuries the route of the rivers, and in some cases even their direction of flow, has been changed several times by drainage schemes. Artificial watercourses, such as the King's Sedgemoor Drain and the massive Huntspill River, join with the rivers to form a complex pattern controlled by automatic pumping stations.

The rivers are embanked, so that roads and neighbouring houses are often well below water level. Whilst the rivers may be unnaturally straight, the roads sometimes meander, because they were originally built on the raised banks of a stream which no longer exists. Water is pumped up from the rhynes into the rivers, which are designed to speed its progress to the sea.

In the past, freshwater flooding was common: some flooding was desirable to feed the rich agricultural land, but it was impossible to control. People just moved upstairs in time of flood. There are tales of rabbits being hunted out of trees and of boats kept moored to upstairs windowsills, just in case. True or not, there is no doubt that floods were an all too regular feature of life.

Large parts of the Levels are actually below high tide level. They are defended from the sea by a broad bank of clay which seems to have been deposited about 2000 years ago along the coastal strip, but this is backed up by coastal defences.

It was not always so, and within historic times there have been massive incursions by the sea. In 1607, what we have learned to call a *tsunami* funnelled up the Bristol Channel and swept across the Levels in a chest-high wave, inundating 30,000 hectares (75,000 acres) to a depth of up to 3.5 metres (12 ft).

As recently as 1811 Glastonbury found itself surrounded on three sides by sea water. Whereas freshwater floods brought topsoil from the surrounding hill country and improved the farmland, the effect of salt water was to damage it for decades, besides the destruction and loss of life such great floods inevitably brought with them.

In the Middle Ages, Glastonbury Abbey had acquired huge wealth and influence. By 1100 it already owned 41 manors and many of them were in the Levels. A large part of what remained was owned by the neighbouring abbeys at Athelney and Muchelney, or by the cathedral in Wells. Do not imagine the monks were all fasting holy men in hair shirts. For the most part they were the younger sons of the aristocracy, and the abbots in particular led very comfortable lives, aside from disrupted sleep patterns. Monastic leaders were by far the most assertive businessmen of the age.

There was no shortage of cash for developing Glastonbury's estates. Drainage was a natural way to make waste land into an agricultural asset, and there was plenty of unproductive marshland waiting to be drained – and enclosed. A statute of 1235 gave the go-ahead for great landowners to enclose 'waste land' (effectively to seize common lands as their own and exclude the peasants) and the Abbey needed no further prompting.

In addition to turning marsh into pasture, drainage projects sought to improve the navigability of the rivers: Langport was accessible to sea-going craft, and Glastonbury to barges – there were transhipment facilities near Rooks Bridge. Bleadney, 7 km west of Wells, served as Glastonbury's port.

After the dissolution of the monasteries in the 1530s, reclamation and enclosure ceased for a time, but in the seventeenth century various get-rich-quick schemes were promoted by unscrupulous courtiers who most certainly did not have the interests of Somerset at heart. There was massive opposition from local people, and riots when reclamation did occur. Similar battles were occurring in the Fens, where the young Oliver Cromwell first made a name for himself taking action on behalf of the commoners against the enclosers.

Vehement opposition continued and no major schemes were put in hand in the Levels until the 1790s. Such opposition was seen from

London as folly on the part of the uneducated. It was true that the productivity of the land as a whole would be radically improved, but in the nature of these schemes only the large landholders and the 'adventurers' who put up the capital did well out of them. Lesser folk were deprived of access to common land, and of their opportunities for fishing and wild-fowling.

By the 1790s, with the population of industrial towns growing fast and the country at war, the demands of the agricultural improvement lobby had become irresistible. Parliament passed a series of Acts authorising the drainage schemes.

The aim, for the medieval monks and for these later 'improvers', was a landscape on which it was possible to pasture cattle for much of the year. Graziers promptly grew very rich, since this land was reckoned the best in England for milking herds. At the back of farmhouses in the Levels the dairies produced 'Cheddar' cheese in summer (some of it was matured in the caves at Cheddar) and in winter 'Caerphilly' much of which was sold in south Wales. (Some traditional cheeses got their names from the places the merchants bought them, rather than

Peat extraction probably began in Roman times, but the industry expanded in the 1960s with the demand for garden peat. As with most extractive industries, it was and still is highly controversial, providing jobs but permanently changing the environment

Meadows flooded in the winter months are ideal for many birds

where they were made – 'Stilton', for example, came from Leicester but was sold to London merchants at Stilton on the Great North Road.)

The Levels today are still a scene of battle between different visions of the rural future. There are large farming businesses who would like the water table kept low so that the land can be farmed as arable, there are smaller farmers who would like some flooding, but access to fields for perhaps nine or ten months, and there are conservationists who want widespread winter flooding, as used to happen for up to six months every year. There is also a peat industry, and the people who depend upon it have their own views on the question.

Because of their unique character, the Levels were declared an Environmentally Sensitive Area, and it is to be hoped that this scheme and its successors will enable a balance to be maintained. With rising sea levels inevitable as a result of global warming, the Levels (like the fens and the Norfolk Broads) may ultimately be impossible to defend. Perhaps a sense of their vulnerability, both to economic exploitation and to the forces of nature, is part of their charm.

Burrow Mump is topped by the ruins of a tiny church, and has splendid views all around. There is a small and rather too well-concealed car park: please don't leave valuables in your car

Athelney boasts only this stumpy monument to the defining moment in British history when Alfred's Wessex defeated the Danes, who never fully recovered. Fifty years later, his successors finally created a united English kingdom

King Alfred and Athelney

On two occasions the Levels have played a significant role in English history. The first was when King Alfred of Wessex took refuge at Athelney after a disastrous battle with the Danes in 878.

At that time, the Levels were flooded every winter, and only locals would have been able to find Athelney, let alone approach it with an army. Athelney was an island, not more than one hectare in size (a couple of acres), with a causeway leading to Burrow Mump, which was a natural look-out point then as now. From that secure winter retreat Alfred called together a new army, and sallied forth to defeat the Danes at 'Ethandun' (possibly nearby Edington) so decisively that the Danish leader agreed to be baptised at Alfred's palace at Wedmore.

In gratitude Alfred founded a monastery at Athelney. It is a mystery why he did not put his money into Glastonbury. Nothing whatsoever remains of Alfred's abbey, and not even a crumb of the burnt cakes.

The Battle of Sedgemoor

The last major battle on English soil took place in a ditch just outside Bridgwater in 1685. James II succeeded his brother Charles II in 1685. He was an overt Catholic, which was not acceptable to the majority of the ruling class at the time.

Although Charles II had no legitimate son to succeed him, the merry monarch acknowledged sixteen illegitimate children. One of them, the protestant Duke of Monmouth, who had already been banished twice for plotting treason against his father, contested the succession of his uncle James. He landed at Lyme Regis and headed for Bristol, gathering an army of sorts on the way – this would become known as the pitchfork rebellion. At Bristol they learned there was a real army mustering against them, and retreated to Bridgwater.

The King's army pitched camp at Westonzoyland. Monmouth decided on a surprise night attack, which might very well have succeeded – but negotiating the rhynes in the dark was always going to be a messy business and the surprise failed. A rout followed. After the battle, the reprisals first by the soldiery and then the judiciary were horrendous. Judge Jefferies is still remembered for his 'bloody assizes'. Many of those butchered were Somerset men.

Ironically, just three years later William of Orange landed at Brixham and was escorted to the throne with almost universal applause, whilst James made an abject retreat. Monmouth was scarcely literate, and Samuel Pepys commented 'he spends his time the most viciously and idly of any man, nor will be fit for anything'. As king he would have been yet another Stuart disaster!

To visit the battle-field, take the lane north out of Westonzoyland and park near Bussex Farm. There is a display board, and leaflets are available. The walk to the battlefield monument is about 800m each way

The market cross   *The tower of St Michael's, on the Tor*

Glastonbury

Glastonbury is a very unusual town – to be honest, bizarre is the word that sometimes comes to mind. Although I like the place, I am not a religiously inclined person which limits my understanding of an important part of its appeal.

Not many places in Britain are seen as a holy site by even one religion, but Glastonbury is both the supposed site of the first Christian church in the British Isles, and at the same time a cult centre for various strands of British paganism. Both my Christian and pagan friends and acquaintances seem divided into those who believe Glastonbury has a wonderful spiritual atmosphere, and those who are uncomfortable with one aspect or another. Whatever your emotional/spiritual reactions, you will almost certainly find it a fascinating place.

The Tor, with the tower of St Michael's church on its summit, stands out against the skyline for miles around, and it is hard not to suspect that it must have been a focus of religious awe from earliest times – though actually there is no hard evidence. A walk up the Tor is a vital part of the Glastonbury experience, if you can manage quite a stiff climb. There is a bus out from the town centre (which is preferable to taking your car because there is no parking anywhere near the Tor) and the walk is then short but steep.

Alternatively there is a very pleasant walk out from the town to the Tor. Head up the High Street and turn right at the top. Take the second left, Dod Lane, and you'll find a footpath signed to the Tor. Continue along a lane. Follow further signs and you'll see the Tor ahead of you.

The main street

The town itself can at first glance seem disappointing, unless you are in search of retail therapy of the mystical kind, perhaps a spot of 21st century cross-my-palm-with-silver, or a short course to 'discover your inner fire-maiden' or get started in alchemy. The main street is generally undistinguished, but with very notable exceptions – a Victorian market cross and two quite stunning medieval buildings, the George & Pilgrims Hotel and the Tribunal.

The Tribunal houses the Tourist Information Centre downstairs, and a small museum upstairs containing displays, finds and information about the famous lake villages. Unfortunately nothing of the villages is actually visible on the ground.

The George & Pilgrims (left) and the Tribunal (right)

A little further up the main street is the church of St John the Baptist, of Norman origin but mainly late 15th century. It has a magnificent tower, the second tallest in Somerset at 41m. Its attractively light interior is richly endowed; the altar paintings, the medieval carved roof and John Cammell's tomb (1487) are especially fine.

Before coming to the main feature of the town, the remains of its Abbey, I should mention two other places to visit, both within walking distance of the town centre but on the Shepton Mallet road, A361.

Somerset Rural Life Museum

A 14th century tithe barn, its size and solidity testifying to the wealth of Glastonbury Abbey, houses the Somerset Rural Life Museum. Farming is represented with displays of carts, ploughs, harrows, a threshing machine and dozens of smaller implements. Other displays include willow weaving, peat cutting, dairying and Somerset's unique 'mud horse' fishing. There are cider and cheese presses and an orchard of traditional apple varieties, where chickens and ducks roam.

The Chalice Well

A little further out, in Chilkwell (formerly Chalkwell) Street, you can find the Chalice Well. The well is to be found in a small but lovely garden, which is very much a place for meditation and contemplation. The spring of reddish water has a place in legend, the chalice in question being the one Jesus used at the Last Supper.

The Abbey's 14th century tithe barn is home to the Somerset Rural Life Museum

The Chalice Well gardens are a place for meditation, and centre on the Well itself (right).

Believers and sceptics will (as usual in Glastonbury) have differing views on when and how the chalice entered the picture, but we can all agree the spring has been in use since at least Roman times, and that the garden (below) is a delight

The Abbey and its legends

Lurking behind a car park in Magdalene Street are the remains of one of England's greatest monasteries. It was probably founded around AD700, and – despite some dark moments including a major fire in 1184 – was supported by successive kings until the Dissolution of the Monasteries by Henry VIII.

Whereas most heads of monastic houses managed to salvage from this episode a golden handshake for their personal future and pensions for their monks, the end at Glastonbury was savage and almost inexplicable. The details of the charges are lost, but the king's chief minister Thomas Cromwell (who was Bishop of Wells in his spare time, so perhaps there was no love lost between neighbours) wrote a memorandum:

> 'Item. The Abbot of Glaston to be tryed at Glaston and also executed there with his complycys.'

The verdict came as no surprise, then! Abbot Whiting was dragged on a hurdle to the top of the Tor, along with two monks, and hanged, drawn and quartered as a traitor. He had probably tried to hide some of the Abbey's property from the king's grasp.

The abrupt end of the Abbey must have had a devastating effect on the town and the area generally. The buildings themselves were used as a quarry for stone, and we can now get only an impression of what

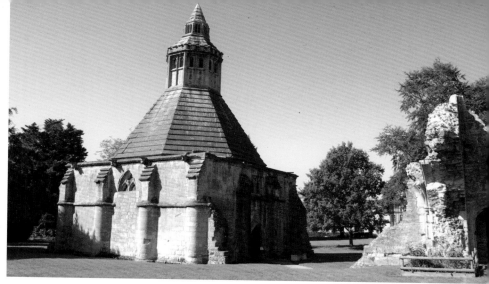

once they were – but it is clear that the church was huge. Although dedicated in 1303, it was never fully completed.

A visitor centre at the entrance to the Abbey attractively presents the history both of the abbey and the town, and the grounds and ruins are extremely peaceful. One monastic building, the Abbot's Kitchen (shown above), survives intact and gives a real feeling of medieval life.

Looking from the ruins of the Choir back towards the nave. A little sign marks the site of 'King Arthur's tomb' which was placed just in front of the high altar

Glastonbury is important not just for what it is, or once was, but also for its place in British mythology. The monks had some very real history to be proud of, but they seem to have been keen to go further. Whether through revelations during prayer, wishful thinking, or cynical opportunism, they developed their early history in several ways: the legends of Joseph of Arimathea and of King Arthur are the two which interest us today.

Nicholas Orme, a specialist in ecclesiastical history, described Glastonbury Abbey in a televison programme as 'the first British theme park'. The monks were quite desperate to attract visitors.

The site of King Arthur's tomb – or maybe not!

Joseph of Arimathea

One of the casualties of the fire in 1184 was a church within a church, a building of wattle and daub which was claimed to be the earliest church in England. We shall never know, but probably it was an early Saxon building.

The legend is that the very first structure here was built by Joseph of Arimathea and his entourage, who came here shortly after the crucifixion to spread the word. Joseph is said to have been a wealthy supporter of Jesus who arranged for Jesus's body to be laid in his own expensively prepared tomb.

One version of the legend suggests that it was not Joseph's first visit, but that he was a merchant who came to purchase metal ores, and that he brought the young Jesus with him. The famous Glastonbury thorn, which flowers at Christmas (or did before the changes made to the calendar in 1752) is said to have been Joseph's staff, which had been thrust into the earth and taken root.

Perhaps with the eye of faith it is possible to take these stories seriously, as either literally or symbolically true. I once met an American pilgrim ecstatic in the belief that the thorn tree on Wearyall Hill was a direct descendant of the one which provided Jesus's crown of thorns. At least it made him happy!

King Arthur's burial place

In 1190 the monks claimed to have discovered the bones of King Arthur buried within the monastery grounds. Even at the time, not everyone believed them. The 'discovery' was highly convenient politically for the king, and a financial lifeline for the monks. The old wattle-and-daub church had gone, so they needed a new draw for visitors – what better than King Arthur's tomb? And it has indeed been good for more than eight centuries of Glastonbury tourism.

But there is a more convincing connection with Arthur than the purported discovery of Arthur and Guinevere's burial: an early 12th century Welsh monk, Caradoc of Llancarfan, wrote that

> [Glastonbury] was besieged by the tyrant Arthur with a huge army, because his wife Guinevere had been violated and carried off by the wicked king [Melwas] and carried thither, because it was a refuge in an unassailable place defended by reedbeds, river and marsh. The insurgent ['*rebellis*'] king had been searching for his queen for a whole year, then heard at last where she was. He mobilised the armies of the whole of Cornwall and Devon; war was prepared between enemies.

Welsh churchmen's attitudes to Arthur were often less than positive, and there is a suggestion here that Arthur was a sub-king rebelling (though with good reason) against his overlord Melwas. Historically the Levels formed a natural border between the state of *Dumnonia* (Devon and Cornwall) and the *Durotriges* of Dorset and Wiltshire. Perhaps Caradoc's story is a folk memory of a war between them, but it may also be the origin of what became, in the legend as we know it, the story of Guinevere and Lancelot's love, which ultimately destroyed Arthur's kingdom. Maybe it is even evidence that the 'real' Arthur actually did come to Glastonbury...

There certainly was a settlement of some sort on the Tor at around the right time (*c*AD500) which could have been Melwas's stronghold, though it may equally have been a religious site: the archaeological evidence was indecisive. Fragments of imported Mediterranean pottery were found there, similar to those found at Tintagel, South Cadbury and other hillforts.

If you want a brief summary of the evidence for or against the existence of Arthur, you might try my own *King Arthur, Man or Myth* (2nd edition 2000, Bossiney Books).

Wells

Wells is England's smallest city (apart from the City of London) and ideal for exploring on foot. The Cathedral and the Bishop's Palace are outstanding, but the Cathedral Green, the Vicar's Close and St Cuthbert's church are also of great interest, whilst the city's knot of old streets offer a pleasing medley of buildings from several centuries.

Medieval statues of kings, prelates and knights rise tier on tier on the Cathedral's wonderfully carved West Front. Inside, the inverted scissor arches immediately draw attention. They were a daring and surprisingly modern-looking 14th century innovation to support the Cathedral's central tower, which was in danger of collapse. The unique branching stairs leading to the Chapter House with its beautiful fan vaulting are also remarkable, as is the medieval clock. This gives a

Vicar's Close, said to be the oldest complete residential street in Europe

graphic picture of the pre-Copernican universe, with the earth at the centre and the sun and stars revolving around it. Jack Blandifers strikes the hours and jousting knights pursue an everlasting circle.

There is much more to discover, for example misericords found under the seats of the choir stalls. These magnificent wooden carvings (1340) show George and the dragon, mermaids, a cat playing a fiddle and many more creatures real and imaginary, all looking remarkably vivid and unworn.

The 14th century Vicar's Close – said to be the oldest complete residential street in Europe – lies on the north side of Cathedral Green. Wells & Mendip Museum at 8 Cathedral Green includes good collections of local minerals and fossils, as well as prehistoric tools, the skull of a bear found at Wookey Hole and needlework.

You can leave Cathedral Green and enter Market Place by Penniless Porch, where beggars gathered. It was ordered by Bishop Beckynton (1443-66). Beckynton also ordered a line of buildings in the Market Place, which have survived in part, plus the original conduit – replaced by the present fountain in 1793 – and the still extant guttering in High Street.

Leave Market Place through Bishop's Eye, also part of Beckynton's rich legacy. Ahead is the Bishop's Palace, protected by a gatehouse and a crenellated wall, all built by Bishop Ralph (1329-63), along with the surrounding moat.

These defences asserted the bishops' authority as well as providing security in turbulent medieval England. But perhaps such isolationism was also provocative: the cathedral front was deliberately damaged by Puritan soldiers during the Civil War and again during Monmouth's rebellion. I wonder whether this was due as much to the alienating effect of the bishop's fortress as to the 'idolatrous' statuary of the west front.

Today, the moated walls offer a peaceful scene. Resident swans have learned to order food by pulling a bell rope.

Stroll along Moat Road to see the Palace walls or enter via the gatehouse (admission charge) for the Palace. Its beautiful gardens cover 5.7 hectares and include a collection of sculptures and the Rampart Walk, with views over the former deer park and surrounding countryside.

Continue by way of bridges to the Jubilee Arboretum and St Andrew's Well. Here an underground river bubbles up through natural springs at a rate of 100 litres per second. This source of water has never failed. Immensely valuable in the past in driving a series of mills, the springs also gave the city its name.

Buildings historian Nikolaus Pevsner described Wells as 'the most memorable of all bishop's palaces in England'. It developed around the residence of Bishop Jocelin (1206-44). Once through the Victorian entrance porch, visitors step back 800 years to Jocelin's hall and Undercroft with their wonderful vaulting.

The Long Gallery houses a collection of bishops' portraits, including the staunch Bishop Ken who defied both James II and William III. Notable too are the collection of bishops' coronation copes and the series of state rooms with their paintings, period furniture and delicate plasterwork ceilings.

Finally, return to the Market Place and walk down High Street to St Cuthbert's, Somerset's largest church. Although retaining elements of the 13th century, it is classic Perpendicular with a magnificent tower and dignified proportions. Among its host of treasures, the carved and painted roof is outstanding.

Market Place (top right) includes bow fronted shops, an 18th century Town Hall and the Crown Hotel where the early Quaker and founding father of Pennsylvania, William Penn, once preached – and was arrested. He was released after the bishop intervened. The gateway to the right is 'Bishop's Eye', that to the left is 'Penniless Porch'

The imposing gatehouse of the Bishop's Palace leads into beautiful gardens, which also provide a wonderful view of the eastern end of the cathedral

A moat surrounds the Bishop's Palace, very peaceful now, but in earlier times perhaps reinforcing the view that the Church was first and foremost an instrument of feudal control?

Cheddar Gorge

Although it is not strictly within 'the Levels', anyone visiting the area should certainly see Cheddar Gorge, one of England's most impressive geological features – over 1.6km (1 mile) long and 113m (371 ft) deep with towering limestone cliffs. Within these cliffs there are caves, characterised by beautiful coloured calcite formations. Stalagmites grow from the floors of the caves and stalactites hang from the roofs.

These caves were inhabited in prehistoric times, and have yielded human remains from 12-13,000 years ago, as well as Britain's oldest complete human skeleton, estimated to be 9000 years old. The mitochondrial DNA of 'Cheddar Man' was successfully matched to that of three local residents. It is likely that prehistoric hunters herded their prey into the gorge, after blocking the upper end, turning it into a massive trap.

Considering its remarkable depth and breadth, it is amazing to reflect that Cheddar Gorge was carved out by water – especially as no water is to be seen except at the lower end of the Gorge, where the Cheddar Yeo emerges from Gough's Cave. This is because limestone is permeable: rainwater seeps through. Dissolved carbon dioxide from the atmosphere makes rainwater slightly acidic. It slowly dissolves the stone beneath, especially along fissures and cracks, eventually widening them into tunnels and caverns.

However, this particular gorge was formed by the abrasive action of water during the Ice Ages, when water in the limestone froze, making the rock temporarily impermeable. Torrents of melt-water scoured through Cheddar Gorge when the Mendip snow cap melted each summer. The erosive power of this river was greatly increased by the scree and boulders it bore. As the last Ice Age gave way to warmer conditions around 10,000 years ago the limestone thawed and became permeable again, leaving the dry valley we see today.

There are several ways to explore the Gorge. The quickest way to see it is by driving up the B3135 from Cheddar village along the floor of the Gorge and stopping in the car parks to gaze upwards. Seeing Cheddar Gorge from above is even more impressive, but the only way to do it is on foot. Climbing the 274 steps of Jacob's Ladder yields the best aerial views, either from the Lookout Tower, or more informally from the cliff edge along the southern rim of the Gorge – please be careful of the drop! Jacob's Ladder also gives a vivid impression of

The Gorge from above, with Cheddar Reservoir in the background

geological time as each step represents one million years and there are information panels and welcome benches on the way up.

For the energetic, various walks on signed paths around the north and south rim of the Gorge offer splendid walks from 5km upwards – the south side being more dramatic. Please keep dogs on leads and beware cliff edges.

As a Site of Special Scientific Interest, Cheddar Gorge is noted for its peregrines, kestrels and buzzards and for the bats which frequent the caves. It is also a good place for limestone grassland and lime loving plants, including Cheddar Pink and Cheddar Bedstraw.

The most thorough way to explore Cheddar Gorge is to buy a combined Caves and Gorge Explorer ticket. This includes visits to Cox's Cave and Gough's Cave, a guided tour of the Gorge in an open top bus and a visit to the Museum of Prehistory. Finally, there are gift shops and opportunities to buy the famous Cheddar cheese. Start from the Cliff Street car park, on the approach to the Gorge.

For further Information: www.cheddarcaves.co.uk   01934 742343

The view from Walton Hill

What to do in the Levels

Relax! It is a characteristic of the area that life is (or so it appears) lived at a slower, quieter pace than elsewhere – a feeling enhanced by the ubiquitous speed cameras on through routes, and the uneven surfaces caused by subsidence on minor roads. Many of the villages of the Levels are attractive, though not especially picturesque or photogenic. Strolling around Wedmore, Mark, Middlezoy or the villages strung along the Polden ridge, or driving round the back roads, perhaps stopping for a coffee or drink at the local pub, is time well spent because they are such relaxing places.

Some places for a short stroll

If you want longer walks in the area (5-8km, 3-5 miles), please see Robert Hesketh's books, *Shortish Walks: the Levels and South Somerset* and *Shortish Walks: Quantocks and Mendips*. If you just want a short stroll, the following may be of interest.

Walton Hill. This lies just south-west of Street. From a parking place beside the road you can walk in either direction along the ridge, with extensive views over the flatlands below you.

Dundon Beacon nature reserve. This walk takes you up to the top of a hill, but this time there are no views. Instead you arrive inside a fortified Iron Age settlement surrounded by trees and grazed by horses. Start from near Dundon's church and walk east along School Lane. It becomes a track. When the track curves right, a public footpath

The Dundon Beacon nature reserve, where you are likely to find yourself the only visitor in a timeless landscape

The walk from Bussex Farm to the Sedgemoor battlefield memorial starts along this track beside a rhyne

is signed ahead, but the track is a permissive path. Follow the track uphill to the right. At the top there's a gateway, with a pedestrian gate of an unusual kind just to the left of the main gate.

Burrow Mump (see page 10). This lies on the Taunton-Glastonbury road, A361. There is a car park on the Glastonbury side, from which you can climb the hill – brief but steep – to the ruined church of St Michael on the summit. If you believe in ley lines, you'll be on one!

The Sedgemoor battlefield memorial (see page 11). This makes a good short stroll from Bussex Farm, on the northern edge of Westonzoyland. Follow the track beside the rhyne for 500m, then turn sharp right on another track for about 300m more.

Langport from the riverside walk. When in Langport, be sure to visit the area near the church, which has a number of interesting buildings including a medieval guild chapel above a town gateway

A few places to visit

This is by no means a comprehensive list, but may help if you have only a day or two for exploration.

Langport is believed to have been a port in Roman times, with a long causeway (now the main street) across the River Parrett and several villas. It is said that the buildings in the main street lean backwards because their fronts are supported by the Roman causeway which is more stable than their rear foundations.

The river is a big attraction, and there is a pleasant walk starting from the central car park and turning left along the river bank, then turning left at Huish Bridge to visit Huish Episcopi's church, with its magnificent tower, and finally walking back to Langport up a street called The Hill. This leads under the Hanging Chapel – a guild chapel – past the church and through an attractive area of the town missed by many visitors.

Muchelney means 'big island' and an abbey was originally founded here by Athelstan in 939. The remains of the Abbey (English Heritage) are quite substantial. The Abbot's lodgings are a complete early Tudor house. Parts of the richly decorated cloister walk and refectory are incorporated in the main building. Tableaux explain monastic life and there is a good collection of medieval tiles and masonry. Outside lie the foundations of the Anglo-Saxon and medieval churches. The monks' two-storey thatched latrine has also survived – state-of-the art medieval sanitation. Muchelney's parish church is famed for the bare bosomed angels on its ceiling.

The Priest's House (National Trust) is a fascinating thatched

Muchelney Abbey includes two substantial buildings, an early Tudor Abbot's Lodgings on the right, and the monks' thatched latrine on the left

The Priest's House, opposite the church, is a particularly interesting building. It is well worth timing your visit to Muchelney to coincide with its limited opening hours – currently Sunday and Monday afternoons in Summer

medieval hall house – with restricted opening hours, as it is someone's home, but well worth visiting if you time your visit appropriately. 01458 253771 priestshouse@nationaltrust.org.uk

Martock is a small town with a number of attractive buildings, of which one is exceptional – the Treasurer's House (National Trust). Built of Ham stone, mainly during the 13th and 14th centuries, the Treasurer's House was so named because the Rector of Martock was also the Treasurer for Wells Cathedral. The house is still lived in, hence the limited opening hours. One room contains rare medieval wall paintings; the hall has a splendid timbered roof and the kitchen a cavernous fireplace. The medieval garden is delightful.

The house is open in summer months, Monday, Tuesday and Sunday 2-5 – but it would be advisable to check opening times before visiting – 01935 825015   treasurersmartock@nationaltrust.org.uk

Meare Fish House   *Westhay Moor*

Barrington Court
This beautiful Elizabethan Ham stone house was completed to a classic 'E' plan in 1559. Owned by the National Trust, it is richly furnished in antique and reproduction period furniture.

Meare Fish House
England's only surviving monastic fishery building, it was built between 1322 and 1335 when Meare Pool was a lake covering $5km^2$, and was probably the home of the chief fisherman: its living quarters were above flood level on the first floor, whilst the three ground floor rooms were used for storing fish, nets and eel traps. English Heritage, open any reasonable time. Key available from Manor House Farm.

Swell Wood near Fivehead, on the A378 west of Langport
This nature reserve is owned by the RSPB. It is a place to see nesting herons in Spring. A wide range of waders overwinter. There is a short woodland walk.

Westhay Moor Nature Reserve
This consists of former peat workings now restored to marshland, and is run by the Somerset Wildlife Trust. Explanatory boards give a good idea of how the Levels may have looked in earlier times, together with clear explanations of their development. There is also a bird hide.

The Willow & Wetlands Centre, Stoke St Gregory
This combines free displays about the willow industry, and the Levels more generally, with willow artefacts for sale and a café.